SPOTLIGHT ON SPACE SCIENCE

JOURNEY TO SATURN

WITHDRAWN

AMIE NICHOLS

PowerKiDS
press.

New York

Published in 2015 by The Rosen Publishing Group, Inc.
29 East 21st Street, New York, NY 10010

First Edition

Editor: Susan Meyer
Book Design: Kris Everson

Photo Credits: Cover (main), pp. 17, 18 NASA/JPL/SSI; cover (small Saturn image), pp. 10, 14, 16, 20 NASA; p. 5 NASA/JPL-Caltech/SSI/Cornell; pp. 7, 27 NASA/JPL; p. 9 NASA and The Hubble Heritage Team (STScI/AURA); pp. 11, 13, 19 NASA/JPL-Caltech/SSI; p. 15 Mark Garick/Science Source; p. 21 Stocktrek Images/Getty Images; p. 23 NASA/A. Tavani; p. 25 NASA Ames Research Center; p. 29 ESA/D. Ducros.

Library of Congress Cataloging-in-Publication Data

Nichols, Amie.
Journey to Saturn / by Amie Nichols.
p. cm. — (Spotlight on space science)
Includes index.
ISBN 978-1-4994-0376-3 (pbk.)
ISBN 978-1-4994-0405-0 (6-pack)
ISBN 978-1-4994-0428-9 (library binding)
1. Cassini (Spacecraft) — Juvenile literature. 2. Saturn (Planet) — Juvenile literature. 3. Saturn (Planet) — Exploration — Juvenile literature. 4. Saturn (Planet) — Ring system — Juvenile literature. I. Title.
QB671.N53 2015
523.46—d23

Manufactured in the United States of America

CPSIA Compliance Information: Batch #CW15PK: For Further Information contact Rosen Publishing, New York, New York at 1-800-237-9932

CONTENTS

MAGNIFICENT RINGS

CHAPTER 1

Saturn is the sixth-farthest planet from the Sun. As it **orbits** the Sun, it is an average distance of nearly 900 million miles (1.4 billion km) from the star at the center of our **solar system**. That's about nine and a half times farther from the Sun than our planet.

Saturn is the second-largest planet in the solar system. If Earth were the size of a marble, huge Saturn would be just a little larger than a soccer ball. This enormous planet is probably known best for the thousands of beautiful rings, made of ice, dust, and rock, that encircle it.

Unlike the planet that we call home, Saturn is not a ball of rock. Instead, it is a massive ball of hydrogen and helium gas. Along with Jupiter, Uranus, and Neptune, Saturn is known as a gas giant because it is a giant ball of gases and liquids!

The Cassini spacecraft captured this view of Saturn from above. Cassini arrived at Saturn in 2004 and has provided many images of the planet, its rings, and its moons.

WHERE DID THE SOLAR SYSTEM COME FROM?

CHAPTER 2

About five billion years ago, the Sun, Mercury, Venus, Earth, Mars, Jupiter, Saturn, Uranus, and Neptune did not exist.

The chemical ingredients that created the Sun, the planets, and everything else in the solar system were floating in a vast cloud of gas and dust called a **nebula**.

Over millions of years, part of the cloud began to collapse on itself, forming a massive rotating sphere, or ball. The remaining gas and dust formed a disk around this sphere. As the material in the sphere became pressed together by **gravity**, pressure built up and the temperature in the sphere's core rose to around 18,000,000°F (10,000,000°C). Eventually, the heat and pressure became so great that the sphere ignited, and became a star. This new star is our Sun.

Gas and dust continued to spin in a disk around the newly formed star. Over time, this gas and dust clumped together to form planets, **dwarf planets**, moons, **asteroids**, and every other object in the solar system.

The Sun is circled by eight planets. Saturn is the sixth planet from the Sun. In this image, the planets' sizes and distances from each other are not to scale.

SATURN'S ORBIT AND ROTATION
CHAPTER 3

Like all the objects in the solar system, Saturn is orbiting the Sun. As it travels through space, Saturn is moving at about 21,500 miles per hour (34,600 km/h).

Our planet orbits the Sun once every 365 days, a time period we call a year. Saturn is so far from the Sun, however, that it takes 10,756 days for the planet to make one full orbit. This means that a year on Saturn lasts just over 29 Earth years! During a single orbit of the Sun, Saturn makes a journey of about 5.5 billion miles (8.9 billion km).

As each of the planets in the solar system orbits the Sun, it also spins on its **axis**. Earth takes 24 hours to make one full spin, or rotation. Saturn is a fast-spinning planet, however, and it rotates much faster than Earth. Giant Saturn makes one full rotation in less than half the time Earth does, so a day on Saturn lasts just under 11 hours.

As Saturn completes a 29-year orbit around the Sun, we see the planet from different angles when viewed from Earth. Sometimes the planet's rings are difficult to see because they are angled directly toward Earth.

BENEATH THE SURFACE OF SATURN

CHAPTER 4

Unlike Earth, Saturn does not have a solid outer surface. The planet is a huge ball of gases and liquids.

Saturn is made up of hydrogen and helium. These two gases are the same

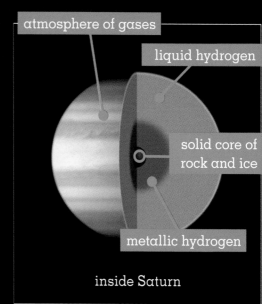

atmosphere of gases

liquid hydrogen

solid core of rock and ice

metallic hydrogen

inside Saturn

ingredients that make up our Sun and most other stars. Nearly 95 percent of the planet is made of gaseous or liquid hydrogen.

Surrounding Saturn is an **atmosphere** of ammonia, water vapor, small amounts of other gases, and ice. Winds in some parts of Saturn's upper atmosphere blow at about 1,000 miles per hour (1,600 km/h).

Storms swirl around Saturn's north pole. This photograph was taken with a special filter to reveal the energy in the storm clouds. The filter makes Saturn's rings, seen in the background, appear blue.

Beneath the planet's atmosphere is a layer of liquid hydrogen. Below this layer, and deeper into the planet, the liquid hydrogen actually becomes metallic, forming a layer of metallic liquid hydrogen. In the very center of Saturn, scientists believe there is probably a solid core. This core may be made of rock and ice, and is about the size of Earth.

DISCOVERING DISTANT SATURN

CHAPTER 5

Ancient **astronomers** watched Saturn in the night sky for centuries. Then, in the early 1600s, the telescope was invented, and astronomers could

Italian astronomer
Galileo Galilei

finally get a closer look at this distant planet.

In 1610, Italian astronomer Galileo Galilei was the first person to study Saturn through a telescope. Galileo saw objects on either side of Saturn. He drew these objects as other planets alongside Saturn and later as arm or handle-like projections on the side of the planet. However, Galileo did not know what he was seeing.

Later, in 1659, a Dutch astronomer named Christiaan Huygens viewed Saturn through a more powerful telescope than the one used by

Galileo would have been amazed to see such clear images of Saturn's rings. This image shows the rings backlit by sunshine as Saturn passes in front of the Sun.

Galileo. Huygens believed that what Galileo had observed was in fact a flat ring around the planet.

Today, with many decades of study through powerful telescopes and visits to the planet by spacecraft, we know that Saturn is indeed surrounded by rings that are made up of billions of particles of ice mixed with rocks and dust.

WHAT ARE THE RINGS MADE OF?

CHAPTER 6

Saturn's rings stretch into space from the planet for a distance of about 175,000 miles (282,000 km). The planet and its system of rings are so vast that it would cover about three-quarters of the way from Earth to the Moon.

The *Voyager 2* spacecraft captured this image of Saturn's rings in 1981.

Saturn's rings of ice, rock, and dust particles are believed to have formed from pieces of **comets** and icy moons that traveled close to the giant planet. Before these space objects could get close to Saturn, however, they were torn apart by Saturn's gravity and pulled into orbit around the planet. As the chunks of ice and rock orbited Saturn, they collided with each other, breaking into smaller and smaller pieces to form dust and particles of all sizes.

This is what it might look like to travel into the rings of ice that circle Saturn. The planet is in the background to the right, while two of its moons are in the upper left.

Over millions and billions of years, these particles gathered to form the icy rings that encircle the planet, held in place by Saturn's gravitational pull.

THE ORDER OF THE RINGS

CHAPTER 7

Saturn's rings are named with letters of the alphabet. It can be a little confusing, however, because they were named A to G in the order they were discovered, not in the order they encircle the planet.

This photograph was taken with a special filter. The green-blue parts of the rings are ice, while the red-pink areas are ice mixed with dust.

This means that D is the ring closest to the planet, and the others then follow from the planet outward as C, B, A, F, G, and E.

Each of the rings orbits Saturn at a different speed, and they vary greatly in width. Ring F is the narrowest at less than 300 miles (500 km) wide. The widest ring, named ring E, stretches into space for about 186,000 miles (300,000 km).

This image shows Saturn's most visible rings. The G and E rings cannot be seen because they are dim and stretch far beyond the planet.

The rings of ice, rock, and dust are separated by gaps, or divisions. The gaps also vary in width, from the narrow Kuiper Gap at just under 2 miles (3 km) wide to the Cassini Division that separates rings B and A. This gap is 2,900 miles (4,700 km) wide.

CHAPTER 8

A moon is a rocky object that is permanently orbiting a planet. Mercury and Venus have no moons. Earth has just one, while

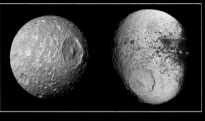

Mimas   Iapetas

Mars has two. All the other planets in the solar system have many moons. Saturn has at least 53!

Christiaan Huygens was the first person to discover a moon orbiting Saturn. He discovered Titan, the second-largest moon in the solar system, in 1655. In the centuries that followed, Saturn's known moon count rose and rose. At the beginning of 2013, astronomers knew of 53 moons orbiting Saturn. There are other objects circling the planet, however, that might in the future be confirmed as moons, and there are possibly more moonlike objects to be discovered.

Titan (upper right) and Tethys (lower left) orbit Saturn. Several moons exist within Saturn's rings.

Saturn's moons have many different shapes and features. The moon Iapetus has a black side and a bright white side. Mimas has a huge **crater** where it was hit by an enormous space object that nearly split the moon apart.

Saturn's moon Phoebe is a round moon covered by craters created by collisions with other space objects.

Enceladus has a diameter of about 313 miles (504 km).

Phoebe orbits Saturn in the opposite direction to most of the planet's other moons. Phoebe is made of very dark material. Scientists believe this moon originally came from the outer solar system where there is lots of darker material. As Phoebe traveled across the solar system, it was captured by Saturn's enormous gravitational pull.

Enceladus is an ice-covered moon that has liquid water beneath its surface. This moon has many cryovolcanoes on its surface. Unlike volcanoes that shoot hot lava into the air, cryovolcanoes erupt jets of gas, ice particles, and even water.

This artwork shows what it might look like to stand on Enceladus and witness one of its ice volcanoes.

Some of the ice particles that erupt from Enceladus's volcanoes become part of ring E around Saturn. In fact, it's believed that ring E formed from ice ejected from Enceladus.

SATURN'S LARGEST MOON
CHAPTER 10

Titan, the first of Saturn's moons to be observed, is much larger than Earth's moon and is even larger than the planet Mercury. Titan has a diameter of 3,200 miles (5,150 km).

Unlike Saturn's other moons, Titan has been difficult to observe because it is hidden behind a thick atmosphere of gases that even today's high-powered telescopes cannot penetrate. Titan is the only moon in the solar system to have an atmosphere. Titan's atmosphere is mostly nitrogen with a small amount of methane. The layer of gases is about 370 miles (600 km) thick, which is 10 times the thickness of Earth's atmosphere.

Since July 2004, NASA's spacecraft *Cassini* has been orbiting Titan and studying the moon. Data from this mission show that Titan probably has an outer layer of ice. Beneath the ice is an ocean of liquid water. Deeper into the moon, there is more ice and a large, rocky core.

This illustration takes you inside Titan, from its surface to its core. The moon's interior contains an ocean (blue) wedged between layers of ice.

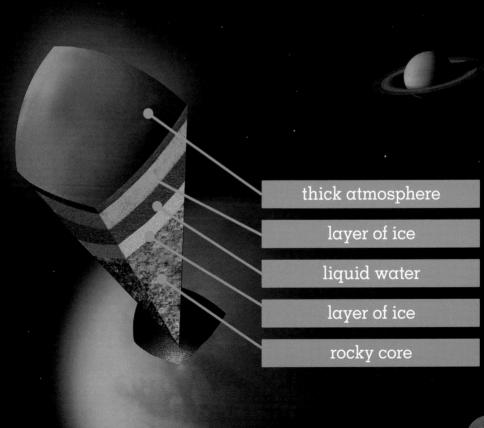

thick atmosphere

layer of ice

liquid water

layer of ice

rocky core

EXPLORING SATURN

Astronomers studied Saturn, its rings, and its moons through telescopes for centuries. In April 1973, the first spacecraft to visit Saturn, NASA's *Pioneer 11*, left Earth on a mission to study Jupiter, Saturn, and the outer reaches of the solar system.

Pioneer 11 reached Saturn in September 1979. During its flyby of the planet, *Pioneer 11* discovered a new moon and the F ring, and collected data that showed Saturn is made mostly of hydrogen.

In November 1980, NASA's *Voyager 1* flew by Saturn. This spacecraft discovered Saturn's moons Prometheus, Pandora, and Atlas. Data gathered by *Voyager 1* also showed that Titan has a thick atmosphere made of nitrogen. Just under a year later, in August 1981, *Voyager 2* visited Saturn,

This image shows Pioneer 11 *flying to Saturn.*

giving astronomers back on Earth another chance to see Saturn, its moons, and its rings up close.

Today, *Voyager 1* and *Voyager 2* are still speeding through space. The spacecraft are traveling in different directions, but are both heading out of the solar system.

LANDING ON TITAN

In October 1997, NASA launched *Cassini*, the first spacecraft to orbit Saturn. *Cassini's* mission was to study Saturn and its moons.

Aboard *Cassini* was a car-sized landing craft called the *Huygens* probe. Named after Christiaan Huygens, the first person to observe Saturn's moon Titan, the probe was destined to land on Titan. Because *Huygens'* engineers did not know what lay beneath Titan's thick atmosphere, *Huygens* was designed to land on a hard surface or on water.

After nearly seven years of traveling across the solar system, *Cassini* entered Saturn's orbit in July 2004. To reach its orbiting position, *Cassini* had to fly through the gap between Saturn's F and G rings! Once in orbit, *Cassini* began collecting data.

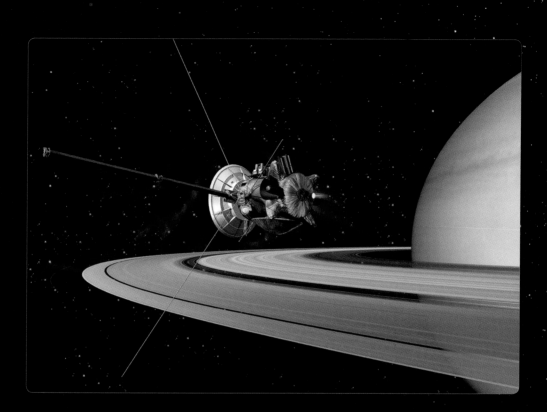

Cassini *reached Saturn after a seven-year journey. The spacecraft was named in honor of Jean-Dominique Cassini, the astronomer who discovered the widest gap in Saturn's rings.*

On December 24, 2004, *Cassini* released the *Huygens* probe. When *Huygens* reached its destination, the surface of Titan, in January 2005, it became the first spacecraft to land on any body in the outer solar system.

Using parachutes to slow its descent onto Titan's surface, from 11,000 miles per hour (18,000 km/h) to just a few hundred miles per hour (km/h), the *Huygens* probe touched down on the surface of Titan on January 14, 2005.

As it descended through Titan's thick atmosphere, *Huygens* transmitted data back to *Cassini*. After landing, it continued to transmit information and images for nearly one and a half hours. Finally, scientists on Earth could see the previously hidden surface of Titan.

Since 2004, the orbiter *Cassini* has continued to send a daily stream of information back to Earth about Saturn and its moons. Today, *Cassini* is still in orbit, and its mission will continue until 2017. Among its many objectives, *Cassini* will look for evidence that the water on Saturn's icy

This artwork shows the Huygens probe flying into the hazy atmosphere of Titan.

moon Enceladus could be home to microscopic life-forms!

Nearly 800 million miles (1.3 billion km) from Earth, Saturn still holds many secrets. Astronomers hope, however, that *Cassini* will continue to unravel the mysterious world of Saturn, the ringed wonder.

GLOSSARY

asteroid: A small, rocky body in space.

astronomer: A person who studies stars, planets, and other objects in outer space.

atmosphere: The gases that surround a planet or star.

axis: The imaginary straight line that something, such as the Earth, turns around.

comet: An object in outer space that consists primarily of ice and dust, and that often develops one or more long tails when near the Sun.

crater: A bowl-shaped hole on the surface of a planet or moon.

dwarf planet: A body in space that orbits the Sun and is shaped like a sphere but is not large enough to disturb other objects from its orbit.

gravity: The natural force that causes planets and stars to move towards each other.

nebula: A cloud of gas and dust in outer space, visible in the night sky either as a bright patch or as a dark patch against other luminous matter.

orbit: To move in a circle around something. Also, the path of an object that moves in a circle around another object.

solar system: The Sun, planets, moons, and other space objects.

FOR MORE INFORMATION

BOOKS

Aguilar, David A. 13 Planets: The Latest View of the Solar System. Washington, D.C.: National Geographic, 2011.

Allyn, Daisy. *Saturn: The Ringed Planet.* New York, NY: Gareth Stevens Publishing, 2011.

Carson, Mary Kay. Far-Out Guide to Saturn. Berkeley Heights, NJ: Enslow Publishers, 2011.

Squire, Ann. *Planet Saturn.* New York, NY: Children's Press, 2014.

WEBSITES

Due to the changing nature of Internet links, PowerKids Press has developed an online list of websites related to the subject of this book. This site is updated regularly. Please use this link to access the list: www.powerkidslinks.com/soss/satu

INDEX